How to
Lie,
Cheat & Steal
Your Way to the *TOP*

www.lazyexecutive.com

IMPORTANT DISCLAIMER

The book presents outrageous and greedy characters totally devoid of scruples, morals and ethics. The situations are fictional and have been grossly exaggerated and distorted for humorous effect.

If you find any resemblance to you or your situation, it is purely a hideous coincidence, which you would be extremely foolish to ever openly admit. Don't worry though… your employees all know who you are.

The Lazy Executive's Guide

How to
Lie,
Cheat & Steal
Your Way to the *TOP*

FRANK ADORANTI

CAPSTONE

This edition published in the UK by   Capstone Publishing Ltd (A Wiley Company) The Atrium, Southern Gate
Chichester, West Sussex, PO19 8SQ, England
Phone   (+44) 1243 779777

First published in Australia by Paperclip Press

Email (for orders and customer service enquires): cs-books@wiley.co.uk
Visit our Home Page on www.wiley.co.uk or www.wiley.com

Other Wiley Editorial Offices

John Wiley & Sons, Inc. 111 River Street, Hoboken, NJ 07030, USA

Jossey-Bass, 989 Market Street, San Francisco, CA 94103-1741, USA

Wiley-VCH Verlag GmbH, Pappellaee 3, D-69469 Weinheim, Germany

John Wiley & Sons Australia, Ltd, 33 Park Road, Milton, Queensland, 4064, Australia

John Wiley & Sons (Asia) Pte Ltd, 2 Clementi Loop #02-01, Jin Xing Distripark, Singapore 129809

John Wiley & Sons Canada Ltd, 22 Worcester Road, Etobicoke, Ontario, Canada, M9W 1L1

Wiley also publishes its books in a variety of electronic formats. Some content that appears in print may not be available in electronic books.

Library of Congress Cataloging-in-Publication Data

(to follow)

British Library Cataloguing in Publication Data

A catalogue record for this book is available from the British Library

ISBN 1-841-12689-6 (pb)   978-1-841-12689-0

Typeset in 10/12 pt Arial.
Printed and bound in Great Britain by T.J. International Ltd, Padstow, Cornwall.
This book is printed on acid-free paper responsibly manufactured from sustainable forestry in which at least two trees are planted for each one used for paper production.
10 9 8 7 6 5 4 3 2 1

Contents

	Introduction	vii
1	Thinking like captains of industry	1
2	Swimming with the sharks	17
3	Managing people in the workplace	23
4	Communication skills	31
5	Showing bosses the respect they deserve	47
6	Optimizing the use of company funds	53
7	Performance skills	61
8	Applying the spit and polish	71
9	Outsourcing responsibility	79
10	Meetings – how time flies when you're doing nothing	85
11	Ultimate plan for success	89
12	Conclusion and revision quiz	97
	Afterword	107
	About the author	109

Introduction

In the beginning...

There is a Scott Adams cartoon where a boss admits to a small gathering of employees that he was wrong in saying for years that 'employees are our most valuable asset'. It turns out that 'money is our most valuable asset. Employees are ninth'. A hapless employee standing nearby says 'I'm afraid to ask what came in eighth', to which the boss answers 'carbon paper'.

As much as you might want to laugh at this, it is my duty to inform you that this is corporate policy at most of the corporations in the world today. Employees are an expendable resource. No matter your position, title or situation, you are fair game as a rationalization target.

Many companies today get the *urge to merge.* The fallout from mergers and acquisitions is the resulting overlap and duplication of functions. Of course, this simply means they have to be rationalized (the process is sometimes euphemistically referred to as 'harmonization') – that is, most of the employees are going to be fired. This is music to the ears of shareholders and investors, and is always a reliable old chestnut to bolster the bonus of a new or ailing chief executive.

This is a guide to staying out of the (ever-swelling) ranks of *uninstalled* or *derecruited* workers. These were the workers who forgot to duck in the face of friendly fire.

This is a possibility rendered especially more likely with the increased use, by corporations, of the 'chainsaw consultant' – that is, the outside expert who is brought in solely to reduce the employee headcount – thereby enabling top management to wash their hands clean of the spilt blood of mass firings.

It is indeed regrettable that we are not given a *how-to* manual such as this one when we enter the corporate world. It would save us a lot of learning the hard way.

Remembering always, that experience is a combination of our own mistakes and what we have observed of someone else's.

You have probably heard of someone (or you may have his/her footprints on your forehead) so apparently lacking in skill, talent or ability who has made it so smoothly and easily to the top. Did you ever notice that, in the process, they effectively steamrollered many others far more deserving and worthy of success?

You must realize that there are people in this world who have no idea about *anything*. In fact, one is forced to wonder how they even continue to draw breath, without an underling having to do it for them.

People such as this have no understanding of the concept of taking pride in a meritorious achievement... simply because they are constitutionally incapable of *ever* achieving anything, on merit.

They *need* to ride on someone's coattails to have any hope of getting anywhere in life. However, their trick is to ultimately convince themselves that their 'talent' produced their 'achievements'. They staunchly maintain such self-deception, even though the truth is apparent to the entire world around them, where the very mention of the person's name arouses howls of laughter.

It just goes to show that if you try hard enough, you will ultimately convince yourself even of the existence of fairies... or, to use an even more far-fetched example to illustrate the point – of the existence of fair and competent bosses.

Did you ever ask yourself how these talentless hacks ever did it? What magical secrets were available to them that were hidden from the rest? How did these persons gain so much real world experience so quickly?

You're about to find out as you read on...

It's because they had this manual to follow. For the first time, these collected secrets of corporate hand-to-hand combat and job preservation will be revealed in detail. Being ruthless and adopting guerilla tactics is the only way you will survive, let alone, get ahead. This is what it takes.

In the corporate world, the saying 'kill or be killed' translates to 'kill someone else's career, or have yours killed by someone else'.

Forget all the airy-fairy, touchy-feely kinda stuff. Let's get pragmatic. These are the ones whose timepiece of choice is the Rolex; the rest must settle for Timex. They drive Porsches; the rest sweat it out on the subway. They live in waterfront mansions and don't know what it's like to sweat (except perhaps while working on their tan, at a corporate-funded getaway).

Their only worries in life are their decisions about whether to go to Aspen or Cortina for their company-funded skiing trip this year, whilst the rest worry about struggling to make the next mortgage or rent payment.

Whilst being cosseted in the lap of luxury flying at the 'pointy-end' of the airplane, they're drinking Dom (as in Perignon) while the rest are contented to slurp Bud (as in Weiser).

Does all this sound totally decadent to you? Do you love the material things in life? Do you enjoy the prestige of being employed? Better yet, do you enjoy a high paying job, whilst not actually having to expend any effort? Do you enjoy living off the fruits of the labors of others? Is it only a scam if you're not into it yourself?

If you too want to firmly thrust your snout into the corporate trough, then look no further. You *are* reading the right manual.

There are four initial steps you need to take, to prepare yourself for the ultimate corporate quest:

1. You have to decide that you want to keep your job (and get promoted) at all costs.
2. You have to decide that you are willing to toss aside any semblance of morals, scruples or sense of fair play that you may have left in you. A fair day's work for a fair day's pay has the same truth and application to the real world as Snow White and the Seven Dwarves.
3. You want it all, without having to work 100-hour weeks and having to sacrifice every weekend for the next 25 years.
4. Most importantly, you have to decide that all the hard work is for the others who get left behind (after all, you'll be the one telling them to do it).

*In short, you must resolve to sell your soul; just **not** to your employer.*

If you elect NOT to follow the advice in this book, you will never succeed; you are destined to spend the rest of your life getting told what to do, by those who do so. You'll do all the work and they'll get all the credit (and all the trappings that follow). Not only that, you'll be destined for the axe in the next wave of corporate downsizing, as a reward for your hard work, dedication and commitment… good huh?

You may be content to bathe in the warm glow of the respect of your peers and family members. You might think that it is more important to preserve your morals and scruples in an unblemished state. That clear conscience will sure help you sleep at night, won't it?

Well, maybe… but none of that is going to make the next month's lease payment on that shiny new BMW you've got your lascivious eye on. Neither is it going to pay for that new yacht you were hoping to park out the back of your waterfront mansion. It sure as anything won't put you within a light-year's distance of a promotion and big fat bonus (let alone struggling to even keep that miserable job, you so thoroughly detest).

Now you have taken the pledge and made the commitment, you are ready to partake of the rules you must observe to get there… there are, in fact, 60.

Some rules are even accompanied by advanced tips (for no extra charge) to help you survive and soar to new heights.

Notice carefully that they are referred to as RULES. Compliance is not optional – they are commandments, which are *mandatory* for your survival. Remember, Moses didn't come down from Mt Sinai to bring us the 'Ten Suggestions' – dare to ignore these rules at your peril.

As an employee, learn to like the taste of dirt

You've heard all about the 'glass half empty' and 'glass half full' kind of stuff haven't you? Well, at work, a more appropriate way of looking at things might be your boss stealing your half glass of water from under your nose, drinking it while you watch, and then demanding you get him more!

If you are a boss, these are the kinds of words you would tend to associate with your staff:

energized   motivated
happy   optimistic
hopeful

Whereas, from another point of view, employees would be more likely to categorize themselves using the following types of words:

angry
fearful   stressed
anxious   self-doubting

No matter how badly you and your colleagues are wallowing in List B, your boss will always consider himself a List A kind of person. There is nothing you can do to change this, so deal with it…

The only way to deal with this situation is to:

- accept that it is your lot in life to be treated like dirt (and learn to like the taste and feel of dirt); and

- religiously follow all of the rules in this book, so that you can (one day) climb out of your hole to become a boss. This will then enable you to dish out, to others below you, the same (or worse) treatment that you previously suffered under.

You have now discovered the circle of (corporate) life.

> "Employees are like violin strings;
> they perform at their best when
> screwed tightly."

Make your company's money yours

All companies have lots of money to throw around. This is a fact of life. If they didn't, they wouldn't have employed you. Right?

Even companies rapidly going down the toilet, have loads of money to waste. Remember the dying days of Enron? Or the legendary rivers of cash that haemorrhaged out of WorldCom in its final days?

With all the talk you hear of companies reducing costs and downsizing, you could be fooled into thinking that companies did not have truckloads of cash to waste.

The only reason that companies go into downsizing mode is to ensure that there is still enough cash on hand to waste on the:

- consultants employed to effect the downsizing; and
- remaining management's ever-increasing salary and benefits packages.

So the cardinal rule here is that: Many companies will waste millions to announce they have saved thousands.

So where does all of the money go? Let's look at where the average company spends its money and then, we will compare and contrast _your_ entitlements compared to those of your boss.

Diagram 1: Distribution of company wealth

1 Salaries and benefits ... 40%

2 Internet charges ... 20%

3 Personal phone calls ... 15%

4 All other operating expenses ... 10%

5 Office stationery for the staff to swipe ... 5%

6 Coffee and biscuits for staff breaks ... 5%

7 Property expenses (rent, utilities etc) ... 5%

The above figures neatly add up to 100%. But wait, there's more! Note that an *additional* 20% (that the company does not have – since it has already reached 100%) is usually spent on needless consultants, to justify the farcical and ill-advised plans of management. Where management is devoid of any such 'clever' plans, they will engage the consultants to devise some for them.

To put it all into perspective and provide further clarification to the chart above, we'll examine below a further breakdown of the single largest expense of many companies, 'salaries and benefits':

Diagram 2: Distribution of salaries and benefits

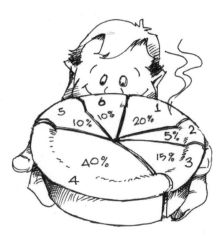

1 Boss' salary ... 20%

2 Boss' car ... 5%

3 Boss' benefits ... 15%

4 Boss' expense account ... 40%

5 All other employees'
   combined salaries ... 10%

6 All other employees'
   combined benefits ... 10%

As you will have learned at school, economics is the study of the allocation of (scarce) resources. These charts above show the results when bosses make every effort to allocate as much of the available corporate resources as possible, to themselves.

You could call it unethical or unconscionable, if you like. I prefer to call it, *welcome to the real world, pal!*

Once you realize that companies *always* have tons of money to throw around, the next problem that you have, is to figure out what you can do to make a large slice of it permanently yours.

You should carefully study the Rules contained in *Chapter 6: Optimizing the use of company funds*, to further develop some ideas on the subject.

" It's not hard to make decisions
when you know what your values are."

Learn the boss' rules

Your understanding of where your boss is coming from and what motivates him, will help you to better understand your boss' seemingly irritating actions.
These are the top six principles that many bosses live by:

- *Never give your employees work in the morning.*
  This will make them unhappy, because they will have the entire day to complete the task – and where's the challenge in that? Always wait until 5:00 pm to bring it to them. They will relish and rise to the challenge of the deadline. It helps break the monotony of their otherwise dull day. They will be reticent to overtly thank you for your consideration and will tend to use irony to show their appreciation. Most employees spend their entire days searching for a plausible excuse to avoid having to go out with their partner or friends in the evenings, or worse still, to waste away the evening by just sitting around at home.

- *Constantly remind them about how urgent tasks really are.*
  If a task is really a 'rush job', you will need to reinforce this to your employees, at intervals of not more than 10 minutes, by constantly enquiring about their progress. They will appreciate your consideration and will enjoy being liberated from the burden of having to remember that you had already told them 50 times that it was a rush job.

- *Help them to become better liked by their colleagues.*
  By denigrating and humiliating the employee for any error or misunderstanding, you will be contributing to their character development and will help them be better prepared for the next time they confront this situation.
  Going that extra yard for them, and humiliating them in a highly public manner will also help increase that person's popularity, by arousing sentiments of

7

sympathy amongst co-workers. Hence, that person will then be grateful to you for helping him become better-liked within the organization.

- ***Do not waste time writing instructions.***
  If you have special instructions for an assigned task, writing them down is unproductive and results in a wasteful and unnecessary duplication of work.

  If you, in fact, save announcing them until the assigned task is almost completed, you will make it far more interesting and challenging for your employees. Besides, it will give you the opportunity to compare your thinking with theirs.

  Your employees have an ingrained desire to emulate and become more like you, so they will look forward to the comparison – if they miss the mark, they will enjoy trying harder, when they suddenly discover that their last few days' work was not what you required and a complete waste of time.

  Take every opportunity to help your employees to become more popular, by using the techniques described in the third point above.

- ***Allow their intuition to develop.***
  If you assign more than one task to an employee, it is far more pleasurable for them to guess their order of priority. Spoiling the surprise and telling them in advance unduly burdens them with more information than they really need or are equipped to handle.

  Never introduce them to people you are meeting with or share the subject or contents of any important discussions. Whenever you later refer to these persons or touch upon any of the points discussed, they will wish to impress you by their clever deductions by actually trying to identify and understand them. If your employees are working hard, they should be attuned to such matters and be able to correctly sense them, without the need to waste your time by having you sit with them explaining matters in detail.

  You will help them in their quest, by assuming that they already have full and complete knowledge of these details. If they fail to make the correct deductions to figure out what is going on, do not hesitate to help them to become more popular, by using the techniques described in the third point above.

- ***Make all decisions quickly.***
  Where it serves your interests to do so, always jump to conclusions without considering all the facts. Ignore the fact that there may be (at least) two sides to a story. The more individuals involved who are likely to feel wronged, aggrieved or just hard done by, the better.

  Never consider the pros, cons, and different perspectives before making final decisions, especially where they might have adverse impacts on the bottom line and employees' morale.

  The only times *not* to make a decision quickly is where a quick decision is needed, or where the decision concerns any aspect of the employee's performance, salary or benefits' review.

" Anything you do could get you
fired; including doing nothing."

Understand the differences between you and your boss

In the daily struggle of trying to keep your job, try to remember: what's good for the goose isn't necessarily good for the gander. That is, do not expect to be measured by the same standards that apply to your boss.

The sooner you understand this truth, the less unjust the whole world will seem to you. Take these examples, for instance:

Table 1: Differences between you and your boss

You	Your boss
When *you* take a long time, you're slow.	When *your boss* does, she is methodical and thorough.
When *you* chat to co-workers, you're engaging in office gossip.	When *your boss* does, she is keeping up to date on current affairs.
When *you* fall asleep at your desk, you're slacking off.	When *your boss* does, she is power-napping.
When *you* miss an important meeting, it's because you're careless and can't manage your schedule.	When *your boss* misses one, it's because someone else failed to bring it to her notice.

You	Your boss
When *you* talk too much, you're a loudmouth.	When *your boss* does, she is a gifted communicator.
When *you* don't do something, you're lazy.	When *your boss* doesn't, she is too busy.
When *you* drink too much, you are a drunk.	When *your boss* does, she is socially active.
When *you* make a fool of yourself at the office party, you are a clown.	When *your boss* does, she is a charismatic individual.
When *you* make a mistake, you're an idiot.	When *your boss* does, she is only human.
When *you* do something without being told, you're overstepping your authority.	When *your boss* does the same thing, she demonstrates initiative.

If you still think that bosses and employees are alike, just take a look at a timesheet for a typical day of a boss and contrast it with yours.

Your Typical Day

8.30 — Arrive at work
8.45 — Coffee
9.00 — Daily planning meeting (AKA first morning snooze)
10.00 — Discuss last/next weekend with colleagues
11.00 — Coffee
11.20 — Surf web
12.00 — Phone friends
12.30 — Lunch
2.00 — Surf web
3.00 — Phone more friends
3.45 — Assemble at water cooler
to tell jokes about the boss
4.25 — Fudge expense account
4.59 — The day's work begins
5.01 — Meet at water cooler to slag off at the boss
for always leaving early
5.25 — Frantic rush to do some work
5.35 — Leave undetected

Your day will contain triple the amount of time devoted to work that your boss' does (your boss usually maxes out their day at no more than about five minutes' real work).

Your Boss' Typical Day

9.30 — Arrives in office
  9.45 — Reads newspapers
    10.30 — Reads reports (executive summaries only)
      10.32 — Coffee
        11.00 — Reads BMW brochures
          12.00 — Lunch
        3.30 — Orders new gadget on expense account
      4.00 — Chats with friends
    4.59 — Gives you the day's work expected to be completed today
  5.00 — Leaves for important 'off-site business meeting'
    (AKA goes home)

" When bosses talk about improving
productivity, they are always
referring to others."

Willingly sacrifice your life and family for your job

Ever wonder why your boss has an ever-accumulating number of ex-spouses? It's usually because he got his priorities right and elected to focus on work, at the expense of his family… that's why he's the boss. Right? Alternatively, the reason for so many ex-spouses might just be because he is a mean and ruthless son of a…

There is a very simple reason why your company expects you to abide by this rule without hesitation or question:

> *You can always find another spouse and get another family – but you won't ever find another job as easily…*

You are expected to dedicate yourself exclusively to a life of work. You must be committed to working stupidly long hours and disregard any other matter in your life for the sake of your work. Your boss' perception of your commitment to this end will, in the end, determine whether you keep your job… or not.

Now is not the time to miss your spouse or your kids. Forget the idea of getting a little time off to go to your dearly departed mum's funeral; forget wanting to visit your child at the intensive care ward in hospital – because you won't be able to even pay for such little luxuries without your job.

Forget the notion of wanting to turn up to junior's (allegedly) important soccer game or to some lame school play – if you lose your job, it will turn out to be the most expensive game/play that you have ever attended. And besides, you wouldn't want to saddle your child with the guilt that it was their selfishness and thoughtlessness that put Dad/Mum out of work forever and destroyed their ability as a breadwinner.

If you care about your family, you will abandon them and be (gladly) willing to sacrifice them for the greater good of your work. That is all that matters.

That is all that your boss really cares about.

Despite however much he might say that he cares, he really doesn't. Don't be lured into falling for that one, for then you will commit the fatal error of complaining, wishing you had more free time, or just pining for your family.

By doing so, you will be demonstrating your lack of gratitude for having a job. In other words, you will clearly demonstrate the disloyalty for which you have always been suspected.

" Work is the refuge of people who have nothing better to do."

CHAPTER 2

Swimming with the sharks

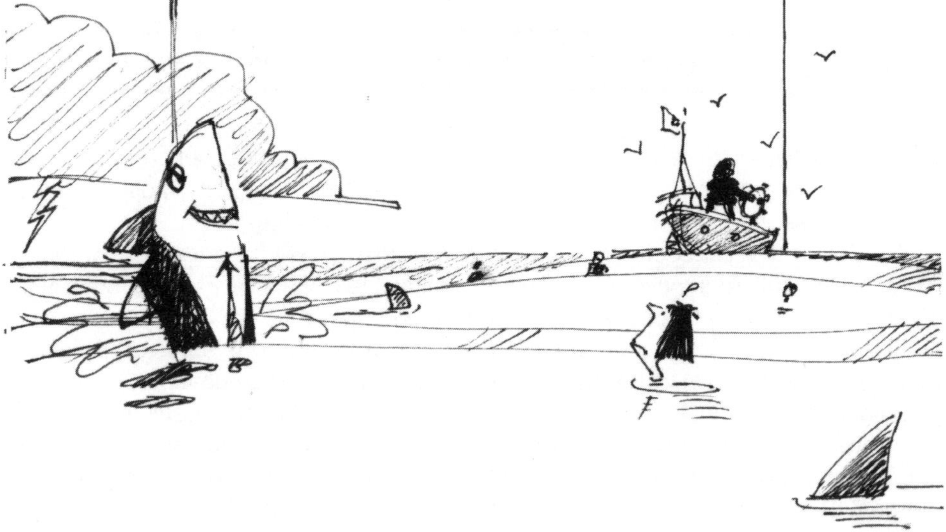

Politics is all about lies, deception and appearances.

After all, politicians don't know how to do anything. They just know how to *sell* the fact that they can do something, even though they are generally pretty lousy at it.

Many less successful corporate executives dread the thought of office politics. Some even allow themselves to become agitated and stressed by the cut and thrust usually involved in the process.

Many believe the word 'politician' to be synonymous with power-seeking, promise-breaking and cynical dishonesty. These, in fact, are the very skills required for corporate survival and prosperity.

If, as a child, you enjoyed pulling the wings off flies (and have carried that passion forward into adulthood), you are really going to have a blast playing office politics.

 Politics and chicanery are mandatory (and can also be fun)

Of course politics is mandatory. If you avoid politics, you do so at your peril. When one appreciates that politics is part of any human interaction, one will readily participate in the process, because it *is* the process by which things happen.

Politics in the office provides you with the most powerful arsenal of weaponry at your disposal. To survive, you need to master their effective use and learn which weapon to use for each occasion where the need arises.

The secret to being a great politician (as well as a corporate survivor) is to never make it *look* like you are playing politics. Power plays must be covert.

Suggestion and insinuation is always far more powerful and effective than an in-your-face approach. More importantly, it also makes it harder to trace back to you. Read Sun Tzu on *The Art of War* – and you will learn that, in many situations, the element of surprise is the best advantage you can ever create for yourself.

Clever office politics should be about five things:

1. networking to build your power base, whilst diminishing that of others;
2. seizing upon opportunities to raise your profile;
3. hoarding valuable information from rivals, subordinates and/or superiors;
4. sidestepping disasters or passing the buck to avoid blame; and
5. taking credit for yours and other people's successes.

Note that every single one of the five elements shown above is a building block of job retention and survival – taken on their own they are insufficient, but when combined, they are a suit of armor, protecting your job prospects.

Corporate politics is a fact of life – either get with the program, or prepare to be overtaken by those who are. As Lyndon Johnson once said:

> *"I'm a compromiser and a maneuverer. I try to get something.*
> *That's the way our system works."*

Well, if you didn't already know, that is the way corporate life works, as well. If you need to do so, have it tattooed to the insides of your eyelids as a constant reminder of your new corporate reality.

> "Anyone who tells you that their company does not have politicians is usually eating their politicians' dust."

Make contacts across functional lines (AKA give yourself a license to snoop)

When you volunteer to serve on task forces and committees you can make contacts across functional lines, to increase your visibility and chances for promotion.

This maximizes your access to the usual networks of rumor mongering that typically exist in corporations. It thereby increases your chances of learning and participating in interesting gossip, as well as general snooping around outside your normal sphere of operations.

Serving on committees can be especially interesting where you get to learn the confidential salary details of others – this can be valuable information to assist you in planning who to target as a tall poppy. It is even better if the details are of persons further up the tree from you.

Once you learn how deeply their snouts are embedded in the corporate trough, you will gain additional inspiration to continue on your climb – the corporate gravy train is a wonderful thing indeed!

Don't worry about having to do any work though.

Most people who volunteer for committees are workaholic geeks and will relish the extra work. You can easily fob off any work to them.

Sow seeds of doubt about your colleagues

Doubt is a very powerful and insidious weapon, when used correctly. For best effect, it must be carefully nurtured and allowed to germinate slowly.

It all starts with a little idle gossip to a boss about 'how things don't seem to be the same anymore' with a certain staff member, or how there's been 'something strange going on lately' with him. How he seems to be spending a whole lot of time downloading stuff from his computer or photocopying a lot of sensitive company information.

The seed is planted – bosses will now start to wonder 'Is he planning to defect to a competitor and steal company secrets to try and ingratiate himself to them?'

A loyal and trusted employee no more – all activities of that person, no matter how innocent, are now are under a pall of suspicion, doubt and mistrust.

This continues until they reach the point where they are openly vilified – the train of thought generally starts to focus into something like this: 'how could he possibly stoop to doing something this underhanded to the company that has given him shelter, fed his family and treated him so well for all these years?'

Remember to distance yourself from such a person immediately.

In this case, you have the home court advantage. Since *you* are controlling the timing of the dissemination of any nasty rumors, you can quietly and subtly begin to distance yourself from these suckers even before you start spreading the rumors. In any event you can prepare and position yourself much earlier than you otherwise would be able to do, if you were simply relying on your political radar to sense that these people were on their way out.

"In a fight for survival, don't lead with your chin."

Be politically astute

There may be some situations where, by an oversight on your part, someone else has beaten you to the punch – by starting the spread of malicious and untrue rumors concerning a colleague.

If this happens, be prepared to react quickly. Alternatively, if a colleague is just a no-hoper and destined to be 'nudged into touch' sooner or later anyway, you must react quickly.

Know when the sands are shifting – if you are closely allied to any one person or group (including your boss) and you learn or sense they may be on the 'outer', you must, do the only honorable thing you can do – dump them… fast!

Do all you can to irrevocably and openly distance yourself from them. Preferably, do so with the speed that a spacecraft must attain to break away from the pull of the earth's atmosphere (or even faster, if you can).

In this regard, perception is everything. You need to act quickly in your denials of liking them, being close to them, or ever having known them – do not wait until the cock crows three times.

Keep the antennae focused on the rumor-mill, gossip and other scurrilous underground machinations that go on as a regular part of life in any large corporation.

Be prepared to act swiftly and move fast – a quick about turn on your part could save your job… and your career.

Managing people in the workplace

Any parallels you draw with dictatorial regimes or leaders will go down well with fellow employees.

An unfortunate by-product of working in a corporation is having to work with other people.

You will find there may be times when you may even have to be part of a team (shudder!). This usually means that you will be required to spend a large part of the day interacting with colleagues, subordinates or superiors and, in extreme cases, having to actually get along with them.

The English dramatist and novelist W Somerset Maugham best summed it up when he once said:

I've always been interested in people, but I've never liked them.

Regrettably, you too will have to do your share of interacting with people at work. In doing so, you will develop relationships with many of them.

To profit fully from these relationships and to extract the most out of them for yourself, you should – ideally – treat these people as you would a spouse or other family member. That is, you must learn to *manipulate* them.

 Be wary of 'friends'

Be wary of friendships developed at work. Friends you depend on at work to support you, can turn against you in an instant, if it suits their purposes (especially if they have also read this book, of course!).

You are well advised to be cordial and friendly with your colleagues, but to keep your distance. Friends at work are not part of your family. They are not people to confide in, under any circumstances and for any reason. Avoid the temptation of thinking otherwise.

The reason being, that money, power, and fierce competition can wreak havoc with even the best workplace friendship. Think about it, if there was only room for one of you, do you think your workplace 'friends' would step aside and allow themselves to be fired, in order to spare your corporate hide?

Sometimes, under the guise of friendship, others may simply want to get close to you to either:

- Exploit you for a 'free ride', as you are seen to be one who is going places, or

- Be able to probe you for information and better determine your weaknesses (and maybe even to be gathering some 'dirt' about you, to be safely stored away and strategically resurrected for use against you, at a later time).

"I've seen honest faces before. They are usually attached to liars."

Beware of the pat on the back

Be wary of any form of overt positive recognition or congratulations.

Your colleagues will not be pleased that you are the center of attention in your department, or seen as the golden boy or girl of the company. Whilst they might offer you hearty congratulations and even offer to take you out after work to celebrate, they hate you.

This is because you have upstaged them – you have made them look like the mediocre hacks they really are, and they will despise you for this.

When you become a tall poppy, threatening to rise above them, their instinctive (and collective) reaction will be to plot against you and bring about your downfall. This occurs regardless of your friendships or history together – for the simple reason that you will no longer be viewed as 'one of the gang'.

You have deemed yourself unworthy of their friendship and camaraderie, by virtue of the fact that you have dared to show yourself as better. An often-heard remark by such people is: "What's the problem with her, weren't we good enough for her?"

> " A pat on the back is only a short
> distance from a kick in the backside."

Keep your mouth 'offline'

It is vital to your self-preservation to 'keep things to yourself'. It is not only the best way, it is the *only* way. *Even if you keep your mouth shut, you've probably said too much…*

Never let yourself be carried away with the notion that talking at length with your colleagues is a good thing. It is a mistake to willingly share all of your ideas.

When everyone else knows what you know, there is no reason to really keep you around is there? Always hold something back. The more you do, the better.

Remember the words of the teacher to the rebellious student:

> *I may have taught you everything <u>you</u> know,*
> *but I didn't teach you everything <u>I</u> know.*

Think about it. This is vitally important. Silence is a necessary part of your survival strategy.

"Never miss a good chance to shut your mouth."

Encourage others to express their views

Your boss is already panicking that her share options may be underwater and that her planned trip to Fiji might have to be cut-back to two weeks: stress is at an all time high.

Now is not the time to complain. Keep your mouth shut, and never *ever* confide about your problems to anyone at work, or anyone who knows anyone from your work. Your boss does not want to hear problems – she wants to hear nothing.

Silence is golden, when it comes to keeping your job. The one exception to this is that your boss *will* want to hear the sounds of keyboards busily tapping.

However, you should feel free to encourage others to stick their necks out and complain 'on principle'. Inspire and motivate them to do so with sayings such as:

"The death of freedom begins with silence", and
"Are you going to stand for this type of oppression?"

Any parallels you can draw between management and infamous dictatorial regimes or leaders will always go down well with fellow employees.

By inciting others to complain, you will be protecting yourself, as *they* will be the ones risking the sack, whilst you continue to be seen by management as a diligent and loyal employee.

Don't ever fall for the sucker question — your boss asking you 'How's things?' Always respond to such a question with 'Fantastic, thanks', even if, at that very moment, your most pressing concern is that your tie and your hair have suddenly caught fire.

" A job worth fighting to keep, is a job worth fighting dirty to keep."

 Confucius says: Never get your meat where you get your bread

This, of course, is a cheeky reference to office affairs.

Office affairs are like playing with fire: spectacular and thrilling at first, but eventually, you're going to get burnt. The result is always certain; it is just the timing that varies.

You can turn this principle around and apply it to your advantage, in the knowledge that there will *always* be those who will imminently yield to the temptation of such forbidden fruit. Even though adulterous affairs are as old as the human race itself, they still retain a certain fascination to many. Why do you think that celebrity gossip magazines enjoy the highest circulation of any publication? We all want to know who's doing what to whom…

With this in mind, you should endeavor to make it your business to know about the extra-curricular sex-lives of others around the office.

These juicy tidbits can be very useful and often career-limiting. All the more reason for you to store away and use such information, in the event that a colleague threatens to leap-frog you on merit or hard-work – neither of which have any place in the corporate world.

It is also useful with superiors – the higher up they are the better. These morsels of tasty information are useful bargaining chips in negotiating a better deal for yourself. In this regard, the implied threat always carries more weight than an overt one.

The value to you of such saucy information exponentially increases with two concurrent factors:

* the rank of one of the persons involved;
* the level of secrecy in which it occurs.

So you can see that it will not work nearly so well with the office Lothario (unless he is canoodling with the CEO's spouse). Whereas, it will be of considerably more value against the ambitious family man, whose career is on the rise.

Avoid a sexual harassment suit

A good start to avoiding a sexual harassment suit is to eliminate the use of these top five, seemingly innocent, phrases in the workplace:

5. I do all the work while s/he just sits there.
4. Could I try out your laptop?
3. Could you whip it out for me before lunch?
2. I want it on my desk right now!
1. What time will you get off today?

Introduce a new layer of management below you

By doing so, you gain two immediate benefits:

- You introduce a category of people more likely than you to be fired, for being redundant to the company's real needs, and

- By increasing the distance between yourself and those below, you automatically promote yourself in the process.

But wait, there's more!

Since you are making the corporate pyramid taller, you help your own prospects by keeping more distance between you and the rank and file – and thereby make it harder for those below to climb to your level.

In medieval times, villages were built high in the hills, to enable their inhabitants to gain advance warning of threats from attackers. It works much the same way in corporate life – the better your visibility of those below, the easier it is to spot threatening behavior. It also gives you the additional time you need to prepare a surprise offensive move upon your attacker (like getting him fired – this is a beauty and always works a treat).

Another fun aspect of this plan is that you now have someone else to treat like a slave and have them do all of your grunt-work, while you take the credit for anything good they might do or inadvertently stumble onto.

Besides, having someone to do all the legwork frees you up for the more important tasks that you need to carry out – like reading the newspapers and going to long boozy lunches (after all, what else is there to do?).

Many books on human relations and business innocently (and quite mistakenly) talk of 'communication skills', as if this was some kind of virtuous pursuit.

You must adapt to a new paradigm – the absolute _last_ thing you want to do is to be known as someone who communicates quite openly, clearly and unambiguously. If you choose to take this route, you will demonstrate to all that your primary career goal is the single-minded pursuit of perpetual unemployment.

If what you say in the workplace is unambiguous and clear, people will actually know where you actually stand on issues. This is career suicide.

Rather than refer to _communication skills_, a better (and less misleading) term might be _obfuscation skills_.

You must disabuse your mind of any conventional notion of communication. You must learn the language of doublespeak and vagaries. That way, you can talk for half a day on a point and no one will ever know your true position and how little you actually _do_ know about _anything_.

This will maintain your flexibility and nimbleness to change with the shifting sands of the political environment. For your career, this is the equivalent of a bulletproof vest.

"Many attempts to communicate are nullified when you open your mouth."

Use the latest buzzwords

Generally, the most reliable way to make yourself appear smarter than you really are, is to keep your mouth sealed tightly shut. However, it is not a blanket strategy you can adopt all of the time, without people starting to wonder whether you have some sort of mental impediment or disability.

On the occasions where keeping your mouth shut is not an option, you will need to be prepared to pepper your vocabulary with a series of the latest and trendiest buzzwords. This will show that you are *au fait* with cutting-edge management thinking and have your finger firmly on the pulse of the latest management trends. It will also deflect attention from the fact that what you are saying is totally meaningless and devoid of any value whatsoever.

Those unfamiliar with your onslaught of buzzwords will rarely dare to question you further – for fear of exposing their ignorance and lack of advanced management training.

For example, the word 'buzzword' is a buzzword, whereas 'getting fired and going bankrupt' is not. 'Six-sigma' is a real buzzword, whereas 'arrested and indicted for corporate fraud' is not.

Buzzwords allow the user to assume a certain air of superiority over everyone else, whilst enabling the user to be insulated from scrutiny. This is because buzzwords are often vague and thereby eliminate the inconvenience of being pinned down to a particular proposition.

The use of vague generalities has never gotten anyone into trouble for rocking the boat or creating discord. Here is a useful collection of some of the better buzzwords (note, that I have not included the meanings of the words, as they are unimportant – what is important is using them):

Invent-your-own mega-buzzword module

Instructions: Take any word from Column A and join it to a word from Column B to make your own mega-buzzword.

Warning: Exercise great care not to actually begin to believe that any buzzword actually means anything or has any influence or bearing on the real world.

Column A	Column B
re-engineer	gap analysis
cross-functional	pain points
move the needle	knowledge transfer
six-sigma	thoughtmap
interactive	methodology
leverage	deliverables
spearhead	resource brokering
streamline	low-hanging fruit
strategically re-align	strategic architecture
mission-critical	bandwidth
ramp up	intellectual capital leakage
offline	asset-base

Column A	Column B
populate	moving forward
future-proof	interface
benchmark	key performance indicators
scaleable	business silo
functionally map	synergies

The more accomplished obfuscator will, for even greater effect, mix and join buzzwords to create *mega-buzzwords*.

Do not feel constrained, however, by the above column divisions; for example, take a look at these combinations:

cross functional leveraging, or
synergistic resource brokering.

More advanced *buzzwordsmiths* could create a third, or even a fourth column, to expand the size of their buzzwords. As with most things, size is something that can be used to great effect to really impress others. For example, a director of a household-name Fortune 500 company was recently overheard to say:

We will need to thoughtmap the key performance indicators for our mission critical deliverables, in order to optimally streamline available synergies.

Allow your imagination to roam wild in the jungles of management-speak. After all, your job (and continuing ability to pay your bills and feed your family for yet another month) depends upon it.

"What you're saying is beginning to make sense; it must, therefore, be time for me to increase my medication."

Keep up to date with information

You can only do so by talking to as many people as you can in the organization and developing relationships, so that you can maintain that flow of information.

Bosses who otherwise have nothing going for them in the talent department (other than a supreme ability to grovel to their superiors), will hoard valuable information from you.

Information is power. Since they have no other talents or abilities to set them apart, they derive their power by selectively keeping information from you.

These bosses are also massively insecure, so if you are seen as being even remotely talented, they will go out of their way to oppress you, out of fear of them being exposed for the incompetents they are.

Such bosses will regularly ask anyone who has contact with you for feedback or comments on your performance. They generally do so by constantly asking others: "How is Joe going?" Of course, the object is always to extract the faintest hint of negative criticism of Joe, to be able to further oppress him.

The reason that such bosses engage in this sort of puerile behavior is because they have nothing else to do in the day, other than looking pretentious and reading the newspapers. These kinds of bosses tend to gravitate to 2IC (second in command) positions, as they are seen as lackeys and sycophantic 'yes people' *(see Rule 48)*. They never question authority above them and never go on to occupy positions of true leadership.

However, they occupy a choice position on the corporate gravy train and milk it for all it's worth. The worst ones are those with delusions of their own importance and ability and actually entertain dreams of becoming directors on the boards of large companies – this eventuality is about as likely to materialize as you winning the lottery tomorrow morning and suddenly sprouting a set of wings.

To counter the incompetent flailing of such bosses, it is important to know the people your boss is likely to be speaking to about you, so that they feel comfortable in sharing with you the idiotic meanderings of your boss.

An effective way to achieve this level of camaraderie is to fan the fires of general laughter amongst employees at the mere mention of your boss' name – "What is it that he is supposed to be doing around here?" Humorous impressions of the boss are good way of adding fuel to the fire:

I've finished reading the paper now. So it must be lunchtime.

Avoid answering your own telephone

Avoid answering your phone if you have voicemail. Don't answer your phone if you don't have voicemail. People don't just call you to see how you are or because they want to give you something for nothing — they call because they want something from you. That something will, necessarily, mean that you could have to expend effort and energy to *do work*. At best, it will still rob you of valuable gossip or web-surfing time during work hours.

Powerful people don't answer their own phones. Ever try to dial the King of Norway, the Pope or the President of the United States on their direct line? If you don't answer your phone, you give the appearance that your time is being more valuably used elsewhere. You are too busy to waste time doing something as menial as attending to a telephone call. High-level corporate strategy is much more important. So is the latest issue of *Mad* magazine, lunch, surfing the web or anything else that gets you out of having to do work.

You can take this one step further; the phone goes unanswered because not even your assistant can answer the phone for you; because she is too busy as well. Wow! The impression this conveys to others is: "This person must be so busy that I shouldn't be bothering them with such a trivial request."

People will always try someone more accessible. They will soon learn to leave you alone. *Never underestimate the other person's laziness!*

Use voicemail effectively, to screen all your calls. If somebody leaves a voicemail message for you and it sounds like impending work, respond during the lunch hour. That way, you're regarded as hardworking and conscientious even though you're being an oily weasel. If you diligently employ this method of screening incoming calls and then returning calls when nobody is there, this will greatly increase the odds that they will give up or look for a solution that doesn't involve you.

The sweetest voicemail message you can ever hear is "Ignore my last message. I took care of it." If your voicemail-box has a limit on the number of messages it can hold, make sure you reach that limit frequently. One way to accomplish this easily is to never erase any incoming messages. A faster way is to leave messages for yourself. Your callers will hear a recorded message that says, "Sorry, this mailbox is full" – a sure sign that you are a hardworking employee in high demand.

It has the pleasant benefit of ensuring that you never have to bother checking your voicemail for new messages, as there will never be any.

Learn your telephone code of conduct

Many organizations have codes of conduct for many facets of the business. This one is a little different – it is for your benefit; or, actually for your survival.

This is the code of conduct to observe when you are on a personal call and your boss suddenly appears from nowhere and hovers around you, eavesdropping on your call. At this point, you need to make a sudden switch to sound like you are on business (as opposed to funny business). Here are some tips to guide you:

What your boss hears you say
   What you are really saying

Please hold.
   Yikes!! I never saw the boss coming.

When did you want to schedule that meeting for?
   What time are we meeting up with the gang?

I was calling about the Friday delivery.
   Wasn't last Friday's game a cracker?

Yes, we're all terribly busy today.
   My boss is currently within earshot.

I need to convene an urgent meeting.
   I'm dying to see you tonight.

Yes, that should be acceptable.
   Dinner tonight? You bet!!

At our offices.
> *At my place.*

I'll get right onto it.
> *I'll start packing up now and leave the office early.*

Thanks for your call, Mr Jones.
> *Can't wait to see you, honeybuns.*

Did you receive the documents I couriered to you?
> *Did you get my resume?*

I am just checking on availability.
> *Has the job been filled yet?*

I would like to enquire about the advertised course.
> *Does it have 18 holes and a bar?*

Is there a possibility of court action?
> *Have you booked a tennis court for us?*

It is important that you circulate the above list to your top 100 most frequently called personal friends/acquaintances. Otherwise, when you suddenly and without warning next lapse into *work speak*, your friend won't be able to figure out what on earth you are saying and will think you suffered a mild brain haemorrhage, causing you to become delirious. That could prove somewhat embarrassing if ambulance officers (urgently summoned by your concerned friend) burst into your offices frantically seeking out the 'stroke victim'.

Be conscientious when selecting excuses for absences from work

As with anything to do with work, you must give your superiors the appearance of being conscientious. This not only applies whilst you are actually at work, but is equally relevant for the days when you'd really just rather not show up.

Being conscientious in the selection of excuses will reap you dividends in maintaining the image of dedication to your job, by cleverly concealing your true feelings.

There are good excuses that have the ring of truth and acceptability to most bosses and there are other excuses that are counter-productive and will land you in more hot water than you bargained for.

Always strive to choose an excuse from the 'good excuses' column. If you are put on the spot and are experiencing a mental blank, do not ever use a bad excuse; for all the damage it could do to your standing, you would probably be better off just 'taking the fifth on that one, boss'.

Good excuses
> *Poor excuses*

I have a medical certificate.
> *I have a note from my psychic.*

I am suffering a temporary bout of aprosexia (an inability to concentrate).
> *The voices told me to clean my guns today.*

I'm on jury duty.
> *I've been convicted by a jury of my peers.*

41

My car has broken down (provided there is no other form of transport available).
>*I was just informed that my car has been recalled by the manufacturer and is unsafe to drive.*

I have the flu and it is highly contagious.
>*I have leprosy and it is highly contagious.*

There is a rail/bus strike.
>*I have been kidnapped and held hostage by terrorists.*

I am attending a funeral.
>*I am attending a rock concert.*

My child is seriously ill.
>*My dog ate my car keys.*

I have an appointment at my child's school.
>*I've been bitten by a snake (which may require the judicious use of a stapler, as evidence).*

I have food poisoning.
>*I have amnesia.*

I have been hospitalized.
>*I have been institutionalized.*

"If at first you don't succeed, cheat, repeat until caught, then lie."

Learn to speak like a boss from work

In order to become accustomed to the cut-and-thrust of corporate life, you should not be surprised to hear certain expressions from your boss and you should learn these, if you ever expect to get anywhere.

On the other hand, some expressions should create a pleasant surprise (if not a cardiac arrest or seizure of some sort) if you were ever to hear them emanating from your boss' lips.

Learn These
> ***Forget These***

You're fired, scumbag!
> *Take the rest of the day off.*

You're lucky to have a job, scumbag!
> *I've decided to award you a bonus.*

You are the lowest form of life, scumbag!
> *We're upgrading you to a company Mercedes.*

If it's not ready by midday, you're outta here, scumbag!
> *It can wait, there's no rush – take as long as you need.*

You're an incompetent, scumbag!
> *Get someone else to help you out on this one.*

You're useless, scumbag!
> *I've given you that raise you've been waiting for… and it's backdated too.*

You're over budget, scumbag!
> *Spare no expense.*

You're never here when I need you, scumbag!
> *You need to spend more time with your family.*

You're a dirtbag, scumbag!
> *You are a highly valued and important member of the team.*

> **"Aggressive behavior is often a good imitation of strength."**

 Always talk about 'adding value'

Bosses who constantly demand to know what value you are adding are often renowned throughout organizations as the ones who consistently and persistently fail to add any value – at any time.

A well-known boss was once asked by an employee, — (whom he eventually fired) "What is it that you actually do around here?" The response was a rather pathetic and stuttering "er… I do a lot of things…er…", to which the employee replied: "I didn't ask *how much* you did, but *what* you actually did."

Great question, but not a politically smart thing for an employee to do…

which explains why he was 'disinstalled' within a few months.

The point of all of this is, if you always *talk* about adding value and constantly demand it of others, it will conveniently divert attention from the fact that you are not adding any value of your own.

Increase your network of contacts and information

Contacts mean information, and information is currency around here...

Do not underestimate executive secretaries and human resource professionals. Make them your allies and friends.

That way you will be included in the water cooler gossip and you may become privy to advance information, such as to who is going to get the axe – so that you have ample time to work on, either, distancing yourself from them, or, devising a creative way to put the boot into them, when they are down.

Part of your power will depend upon the network of contacts you have developed (both inside and outside your company) and on the volume and quality of information flowing in to you.

Internal confidential memos usually contain the juiciest and most destructive news. You would do well to remember that confidential memos are typed by secretaries...

Just think of the trillions of dollars that would be saved by downsizing away all of the incompetents in the corporate world.

On the other hand, imagine the stratospheric unemployment rate amongst your former bosses and the consequent 'leadership' vacuum we would inherit!

Never underestimate the power of grovelling over competence and merit. The world revolves around incompetence. Remember that God must really love incompetent bosses – because he made so darn many of them!!

Learn the art of assmosis

The method by which some people get ahead by sucking-up to the boss, rather than on merit or hard work, is scientifically referred to as *assmosis*. If your boss is a dope, you will need to learn this skill to survive.

The best place to observe this phenomenon is to watch your boss sucking up to his boss.

Carry out any such observation with great care though, as your boss' groveling will be guaranteed to be highly embarrassing, if not downright sickening.

Such displays of sycophancy are ideally best dealt with by administering repeated sharp blows to the back of the skull using a precision object, such as a computer printer or large-screen monitor.

However, it is not a recommended panacea, due to its (often) career-limiting effects.

"You can lead a fool to wisdom but you can't make him think."

Never upstage or outshine your boss

If you can outdo your boss by simply breathing and maintaining a steady pulse…
then don't.

Your goal should be to always make your superiors feel… er… superior. Even if
they possess the intelligence of an earthworm (as they often do, together with the
morals of a scorpion!), you need to challenge yourself to find ways of making them
look good. In many cases this is about as easy as performing brain surgery… with
your feet, whilst blindfolded – but it can be just as rewarding.

Many think that displaying their talents and abilities to their superiors will serve
to draw their awe and admiration. Wrong! It will only serve to highlight the fact to all
around them that the boss is nothing more than a waste of space (and oxygen) – it
will make them feel even more insecure than they already are.

Do not overachieve

If you do, it will set you apart from your colleagues – this means you'll get noticed by
them. This, of course, is the last thing that you want. You do not depend upon your
colleagues for your continuing employment. Hence you should not need or want to
impress them in any way.

If you do so, your colleagues will sense that you are becoming a tall poppy and
will do all they can to ensure that they do the only thing that should be done to tall
poppies – cut them down without mercy.

They will plot, collude and plan to sabotage you.

Your boss is the only person you need to impress.

"Friends may come and go, but
enemies just seem to accumulate!"

Be a work slave

Remember you do not have feelings, self-esteem or self-worth. At work, you are not yourself. You are an automaton – programmed only for work and following your boss' bonehead commands.

Forget any feelings of appreciation for a job well-done or the prospect of deriving any semblance of personal fulfilment on the job.

"Just concentrate on being the best
slave you can be."

Carry out an unpleasant task for your boss

This is a great thing to do, especially if the task is firing someone or, better still, a large group of hapless workers.

Firstly, you will become your boss' right hand man – read that as meaning indispensable (a key to keeping your job).

Secondly, and most importantly, it will raise your profile, stature and perceived importance within the organization – 'Goodness, I didn't know Bob had the authority to fire people!'

Take great care in the precise manner and wording you use when declaring yourself available to carry out an unpleasant task for the boss, lest you find yourself having to assist in one of their regular applications of Preparation H or, worse still, having to go out for a drink with them.

Be supportive of your boss

Offer to help control costs. Offer to help write about departmental accomplishments. This could give you a license to snoop on other people's doings in the organization and may increase your exposure to sensitive information. It can be a valuable source of dirt on your colleagues.

Best of all, it keeps you away from the mundane tasks of your own job.

Don't get too close to your colleague – especially if the sands start to shift away from her. Be prepared to distance yourself from her quickly if need be (for example, if you hear some juicy HR gossip that she's fallen out of favor with those that matter or, better still, about to be axed).

You'll need that same gossip network to find out who the replacement is going to be (before your colleagues find out) so that you can position yourself ahead of them and, if necessary, plant the seeds with that new boss of any gossip and negative information about a tall poppy (or a potential one).

This is especially powerful because if you do so before the replacement is officially announced, it will be viewed as genuine and believable and not for the shameless power play that it is.

Become a valued coach and mentor

By helping others, you are adding value.

Mentoring is currently one of the 'hot' trends that companies are currently experimenting with. It is seen as helping transmit job skills and reinforcing the company culture as caring and nurturing – the idea being to build a more cohesive workforce.

As a confidante, the upside of this for you is that it gives you the ability to know who is most fearful of their jobs being axed. If they have something to be fearful of, then they must have good reason to be scared. It is your moral duty to your company to systematically find and weed these people out.

This can provide you with valuable information to help turn their fears into reality – as everyone knows, the best way to conquer your fear is to confront it.

Not only are you helping the company, but you are actually doing these people a favor in their own personal development. One day they will thank you – just make sure they never actually find out that *you* are the one to whom they owe their thanks…

"You shouldn't automatically expect to be respected at work. You need to get down on your knees and beg for it."

We have already established the fact that companies have lots of money to throw around – the trick is how to make most of it yours. Your imagination and chutzpah should be the only limiting factors.

It is morally wrong to allow a company to keep all of its money.

The company would just waste it on pointless expenses, anyway. The idea is to save the company from doing so, by taking away the funds it would waste. Remember that your boss already stays awake at nights plotting to do the same thing… you are in a race – *before* the money runs out.

The rules below are just a primer with the corporate petty cash tin, until you graduate and are ready for the big league, using the ultimate plan for success set out in *Rule 59* (don't skip to it just yet, as you will be unprepared and ill-equipped to appreciate and extract its full benefit).

Trim excesses from budgets and expenses

Trim excesses, preferably from the budgets of *others*.

That is why it is important to have a license to snoop (*Rule 7*) and to be seen as a mentor to others (*Rule 31*). This gives you valuable information to help identify areas for cuts to be implemented.

As you become known for your value in identifying areas for saving, you will be seen to be increasingly valuable to the company's bottom line – even if you are personally despised.

Consequently, your own expenses will draw less focus and attention because of your increase in value to the company.

Host events at your company's expense

Your number one goal is to build your profile. Hosting lavish events with your industry group and/or peers is often a good way to do so. The more lavish these events are, the better.

Spare no expense in hosting networking and other events of your network group or professional association – but only do so at your company's expense.

Use the best boardrooms and the most lavish catering facilities. Remember that money is no object – of course not, it isn't yours.

Buddy up to your customers

Take customers to long boozy lunches or better still, use corporate funds to purchase the best seats at the most prestigious sporting events. Naturally, you will need to accompany the customers as the representative of your company.

Extensive use of this tactic will lead you to being viewed by the customer as their relationship contact.

If you are liked and sought after by your organization's customers, your position is solidified.

This transfers the focus onto someone else less valuable, to be more likely considered for the chop.

Cut prices to important customers

This is an extension of buddying up to them. Be liberal – this is the company's money not your own.

Caution – this tactic can be a double-edged sword. Some customers will see you in a better light and you may even make it onto their hiring radar. Others, however, will see an unsolicited price-cut as a sign of weakness and of a negotiator failing to protect the interests of their master.

For that reason, you need to carefully size-up your customer, to ensure that they fall into the former category, before pulling such a stunt.

Remember that the sole reason for doing so, is bolstering your own personal position at the expense of your company.

If the worst happens and you are headed for the chop, extensive use of the above methods *before* news of your fate is officially known, could be a useful networking 'hook' for you, ultimately leading to employment with one such customer.

Remember: The key to this method is the liberal use of the tactic, coupled with extensive and lavish gift-giving and other perks – under the guise of customer relations.

Be innovative with your expense account

Remember that it is your moral duty to do so – otherwise the company will be forced to fritter the money away on wasteful things (such as someone else's expense account).

You need to be both creative and innovative in the methods you use and the excuses used to justify personal expenses as corporate ones. Remember that (allowing for the effect of taxes), every dollar you spend in personal expenses on your expense account has the same benefit to you as adding two dollars to your gross salary. Go for it!

Following are some introductory tips, however, a word of *caution* first – do not regard these tips as setting limits on what you can achieve with careful planning. It is best to regard them as a springboard for your imagination…

Expense claim primer

Staple items include mobile phones

Always aim for the most upmarket models. Don't just stop at one, however. You will need a spare (just in case), a world phone (in case you travel), one for your spouse and enough for all your kids.

Another useful addition to your home office is an extra notebook computer

You can use any excuse for your old one – stolen out of your car, left at the airport, left in a cab etc. Or, an award-winning way to do it is to claim that the battery or other key component has died and that they are no longer available. As soon as you order the new computer, you can easily obtain the replacement battery from another source (such as eBay) and, *voila*, you have another fully functional notebook available for a family member!! Be sure to do the upgrade only when the new models are released to ensure that you have the latest and greatest to brag about.

Do not be remiss in failing to have your fill of extravagant lunches at the company's expense.

Take all of your friends and acquaintances, as well as using it for any networking opportunities. If enough of your friends are also doing this with their expense accounts as well, you can set up a roster system to ensure that you will never need to demean yourself with a brown bag lunch, for as long as you live.

As they are 'client' lunches, you will be expected to impress and not hold back on your selection of expensive wines: aim for bottles with grand sounding names like Chateau Lafite Rothschild, Grange Hermitage, Krug and Dom Perignon – the older they are the better, of course. You too can experience the taste of bottles that cost more than most people earn in a week!

Motor vehicles

If you have a fully maintained company car, then ensure that your other car at home is also routinely fuelled and maintained at the company's expense.

Client entertainment is usually a reliable old chestnut to use for any other miscellaneous expense such as household groceries, season football tickets – under this guise, you can claim virtually anything; even the mooring expenses on your boat. If you don't have a boat, you might want to think about a way that you could get away with purchasing one on your expense account…

Make effective use your 2IC's expense account

For problem expenses such as your flying lessons or that $15,000 feng shui study you've just had done on your hobby farm, you'll need to work out an arrangement with your sycophantic 2IC.

An old trick is to have your 2IC book up to his expense account the most outrageous expenses you can dream up – which, of course, *you* then get to approve.

Sometimes, due to the sheer magnitude, outrageousness and flagrant audacity of such expenses, there is every risk of a disgruntled underling blowing the whistle on you and blabbing to head office. This is especially more likely to occur when your

2IC takes pleasure in disallowing the most minor and inconsequential staff expenses on items such as a single postage stamp, a small box of paper-clips or a stick of gum in lieu of a meal – for lack of proper receipts or proper sign-off approval.

If head office were to ever query you on your outrageous expenses, you could then act totally righteous and indignant by pointing to the strict and mean way that your employees' expenses are routinely scrutinized and disallowed.

If that doesn't work, you could fire the 2IC for incompetence – an absolute cinch to make out and *totally* believable. Of course, you would need to fire the 2IC very quickly, *before* anyone from head office asked too many questions. The 2IC's mouth will be guaranteed to stay shut, especially considering the oversized severance package they'll be walking away with (awarded by you) – and the fact that 2IC gets to come back again as a retained consultant.

Now that's what I call win–win!

There are certain skills in which you need to become proficient and well-versed. They are not commercial or financial skills. Nor are they oral or verbal expression or presentation skills, in the normally understood sense.

It is all about presentation of a *performance*. The word *performance* is used in the theatrical sense – that is, it is fictional and contrived – that's right, fake!

Just like your company's financial statements…

Make the small volume of work expand to go beyond the available time

When confronted with a two hour task…only a fool would attempt to complete it within that time or – perish the thought – in even less time.

Remember, in order to keep your job, your primary objective is to appear busy and essential. If you have nothing to do, you will hardly be seen as essential – unless you are the boss, of course – in which case it doesn't really matter.

If you stupidly (or perhaps accidentally) complete a task within the time allotted, this will simply mean that you will be given something else to do – yes, that's right, more work! Yikes!!

You must dedicate yourself to carefully crafting your tasks so that you can:

- involve as many others as possible in performing the task (after all, it is highly complex isn't it?);
- blow-out the time required for the task; and
- blame external circumstances or, better still, the others involved for the delays (this is usually the effective outcome of a *blamestorming* session).

Remember that the first 90% of a project takes up to 90% of the allotted time, whilst the last 10% takes up the other 90% of the time.

"The payoff for laziness is immediate."

Work the 'right' hours

Most bosses are real *olde worlde* 'quill and ink' types. What do you think a typical boss prefers to see in their staff:

1. Someone who can get a whole day's work done by lunchtime, does an extra day's work by 4 pm and is out the door by 4.30 pm?, or
2. A plodder who spends 14 hours a day in the office to barely accomplish half a day's work?

That's right. The plodder who is seen at their desk wins every time. Note that the plodder is the personality type that a boss more closely relates to...

Productivity has absolutely nothing to do with it.

Getting to work early may not help you if the boss is one who stays late. You will not be 'seen', and therefore will not be thought of as a 'conscientious worker' – this is not a recipe for keeping your job.

Bosses tend to measure performance by how full the car park is at 7 pm – this is more reflective of the typical attitude in the corporate world.

Remember that all bosses expect their staff to work *some* unpaid overtime: *some* every night and *some* every weekend.

"It doesn't matter what you do, it only matters what you say you've done and what you say you're going to do."

63

(Pretend to) work longer hours

This does not conflict with any other principle stated in this book. It depends on how you make it appear, not what you do.

The key is to make sure that you are *seen* to be spending more time working, but not necessarily doing more work. This may sound confusing but it's actually quite simple.

Bosses are simple creatures – many will measure the productivity of their staff by the number of cars they see in the parking lot late in the evening. This shortcoming in their character should alert you to another clue – whenever you can, bum a lift from colleagues and leave your car in a prominently visible space in the corporate parking lot.

This way, your boss (or any other overachiever) will notice your car, regardless of how late they leave work, or how early they get there.

"If you are good, you will be assigned all the work.
If you are really good, you can successfully avoid any work."

Send emails at odd hours

It is a critical investment of your time to learn the ways to configure your email program to defer sending emails until more impressive looking times. For example, an email that was composed at 10 am can be delayed until 3.30 am.

Do not use this tactic *too* liberally. Like any clever tactic, it should be used strategically and sparingly – with those who count. After all, you don't want everyone to begin to wonder whether you are even in the office at all during the day.

Its use should be restricted only to superiors of strategic importance to you. If you use it with your colleagues, they will become suspicious that you are setting yourself apart from them by outworking them and they will seek to undermine you.

Walk around the office with documents in your hands

People with documents in their hands look like hard working employees heading for important meetings. The best way to achieve this look is to use the trusty old folder.

These can be filled with your favorite magazines, your personal tax return details, home budgets, print outs of your favorite dirty jokes emailed by your friends etc.

The three rules to observe about holding documents:

1. People with nothing in their hands look like they're heading for lunch.
2. People with only a newspaper in their hands look like they're heading for the bathroom or the betting shop.
3. People holding what *appear* to be important documents in their hands look like they're heading for the boardroom. Even better if the folder has the words CONFIDENTIAL conspicuously stamped on the front.

A real pro will have the words **HIGHLY CONFIDENTIAL** stamped *in red* on the front of any folder they are carrying. Naturally, if anyone attempts to seek a closer look at what you are carrying, those magic words act as a shield to prevent prying eyes from discovering what they are really up to – with the latest edition of *Sports Illustrated* or *Vanity Fair*...

> " When you have nothing to do
> (or don't actually know what it is
> that you should be doing), carry
> documents, walk fast and look
> worried."

Carry bundles of seemingly important-looking documents when you leave the office

You must ensure you always carry loads of stuff home with you at night.

This is extremely easy if you drive to and from work. You should actually get into the habit of keeping a stash of useless (but important looking) documents in the back of your car. They can be at hand if you arrive at work at the same time as your boss. You innocently ask him to help you carry 'last night's papers' into the office. This is particularly effective if you look like you've been up all night reading them (they'll never guess that the time was actually spent in a seedy all-night bar or club).

This is a necessary tactic to generate the false impression that you work longer hours than you do (because, of course, you actually do no work at all).

If you do it often and well enough, you'll actually be asked to 'take some time off and relax'. Of course, as a good corporate soldier, you reluctantly allow your arm to be twisted and accept such an offer.

Of course, if you are a superstar, you will ensure you are seen coming to the office from your 'day off' with another load of papers.

"The facts, although generally interesting, are irrelevant."

Use your computer to appear busy

Any time you stare intently and thoughtfully into your computer, you look like you are working, to the casual observer.

You can send and receive personal email, calculate your finances, place bids on eBay, or just generally have a blast without having to do anything remotely related to work. These aren't exactly the societal benefits that everybody from the computer revolution expected, but they're pretty good nonetheless.

If you are ever asked by your boss why you are spending so much time on the computer, your best defence is to say: 'I've been checking out some interesting stuff about our competitors.' As you are promoting and furthering the company's interests, you will be seen as a motivated self-starter. If your boss is over 21 years of age, you can be assured that he or she will not be the slightest bit computer literate (or nowhere near as web-savvy as you are) so you have a serious degree of latitude to use some license with your excuses.

If you're a real pro, you can offer to demonstrate some of your new discoveries. That will make your boss scurry away like a frightened salamander.

Never turn your back on your co-workers

You must do everything in your power to ensure that your screen or your desk is not visible to anyone walking past your office or work area. This will minimize the chances of you being detected doing something other than work.

The easiest way to do this is to claim that facing away from the door/corridor is bad feng shui and could make you seriously ill.

You must always be facing the door to your office so that you have plenty of advance notice of the approach of someone. This will give you ample time to undetectably switch from your favorite internet site to your pre-arranged screen full of words or figures (that you actually did in the days before you read this book). Or it will allow you sufficient time to cover up this month's tips on dating with this month's financial projections.

It is a valuable investment of your time to learn and practice the 'computer-screen-switch' and 'magazine cover-up' as often as you can, to the point that you can instinctively and imperceptibly switch or cover-up when the pressure's really on! That is, when you're so deeply engrossed, you don't see the chairman of the board stroll in; you only have a split-second to react.

"Friendly fire isn't."

Expand your skills' base

Become known for your skills as an amateur photographer. This is a corollary of the license to snoop.

For this reason, it pays never to be drunk at parties – your only reason for being at corporate parties is for reconnaissance and to gather intelligence on the enemy.

The party atmosphere and alcohol are usually enough to loosen the inhibitions of most; and that's when you come in…

You can now gather hard evidence that will make you a feared and respected player and powerbroker – especially amongst the more lecherous of your colleagues and superiors.

Information is power – and you now become the keeper of their grubby little secrets. You will be protected and safeguarded by those who fear your newfound knowledge.

CHAPTER

8

Applying the
Spit and Polish

Keeping your job is like applying for a bank loan. You are more likely to be successful if you have the appearance of not needing it in the first place.

If you aspire to upper management, you at least need to prove that you would fit in and look the part – understand this now; talent has absolutely nothing to do with it. If it did, the boardrooms around the world would look like long-abandoned ghost towns.

Surround yourself with the right trappings

In maintaining the image of aspiring upper management, you will need to project the appearance of understated authority and importance. To do this, there are a number of fundamental accessories to consider.

Style counsel – the short-form version

Suit

The key here is to avoid any fabric that sounds like the chemical composition of fast-food. Go for natural fibres such as wool and strive for a look of understated elegance (that means no polyester or poly-anything!). For women, look for names like Valentino, Chanel and Armani. For men, look for names like Chester Barrie, Zegna, Caruso, Brioni etc.

Shirt

Well cut and crisp with French cuffs and appropriate cufflinks. Pure cotton is the way to go here for comfort and wearability, although by 10 am, it will look as though you slept and showered in it. Look for Hardie Amies, Gieves & Hawkes etc.

Tie

Again the key is elegance – and silk is the only fabric (no nylons!). It is preferable that they be made by textile workers, rather than industrial chemists.

Shoes

Leather and Italian are always a good combination. For women, look for Prada or the legendary Manolo Blahnik (immortalised in the TV show *Sex and the City*). For men, John Lobb makes a very fine shoe, provided you have sufficient equity in your home to take out a second mortgage. Or, you could try buying one shoe at a time, after each lottery win…

Briefcase

When it comes to briefcases, size is important. Unlike other areas in your personal life, smaller and thinner is better. The image to project is that since you are only concerned with 'big-picture' issues, there is no need for you to lug home crates of documents. These are the province of those lower down the corporate tree. Besides, since you are doing all that you possibly can to actually avoid any semblance of work, you don't really need a commodious briefcase. As long as you can fit in a nice pen and a copy of this book, you really have all that you could possibly ever need to succeed at work.

Pen

This is your chance to shine. Forget the chewed-up plastic disposable or even the ubiquitous plastic (sorry, I meant resin) wannabe prestige brands littering the corporate battlefields of the world. We're talking about a nice (and none-too-common either) Montegrappa or Visconti, preferably a limited edition. It must be chunky, needing at least 2 hands to hold it. And please, don't chew (or otherwise salivate) on the end of it!

Notebook computer

This can be a sure-fire status symbol – however, it must be sexy. This means either, the absolute latest-and-greatest Pentium or, better yet, an Apple aluminum PowerBook. Size matters here too – it must either be really teensy and wafer-thin (12 inch screen or less) or absolutely humongous and wafer-thin (17 inch screen or greater).

Wristwatch

The old multi-function plastic-cased digital timepiece with barometer, inclinometer, calculator and metric converter doesn't really tell the world you are ready for the big league. You need to focus on heavyweight brands: Rolex, Omega, Patek Philippe, Piaget, Breguet etc. For women, the only choices are two models by Cartier – the Panthere and the Tank Français (both in gold). For men, you will need to make two choices of style: firstly whether to go for the simple and ultra-thin look (such a Patek) or a chunky chronometer style (such as the Rolex Daytona); the second choice is whether to 'go for the gold' or opt for the 'poverty model' in stainless steel.

Provided you assiduously follow the steps detailed above, you should never embarrass yourself amongst the style-conscious at the apex.

Ensure that your own 2IC is a dunce

Most, if not all, astute CEOs religiously follow this rule.

One way of presenting yourself as a good employee is to have mediocre or downright terrible employees surrounding you.

There are a number of good reasons for doing so. Firstly, you will be seen to be better than you really are, since it will not take much candlepower on your part to massively outshine your 2IC.

Better yet, your boss (or your board, if you are the CEO) will be better able to resist the (ever-present) temptation to fire you.

Your ideal 2IC is one who rules those below like a medieval despot using a cast iron fist, and on the other hand, is grossly obsequious and slavishly sycophantic to you. The trick is to have a *loyal* dunce as your deputy (or, at least, one who does not have the mental horsepower to ever plot against you). The going price of loyalty these days is a fully maintained 3 Series BMW.

Ever notice that many 2ICs are much older than their bosses – this is by design, since age takes away the will or opportunity for any ambition to ever want to leapfrog the boss. In fact, such 2ICs are at an age where they are probably unemployable elsewhere, and they know it.

Note carefully, however, if you are ever pressured from above to hire a strong 2IC, you should see this as being the writing on the wall; you're going down (see *Rule 18*).

"A person who can't lead and refuses
to follow makes a useful roadblock."

Never have a tidy desk

Only top management can get away with a clean desk. For everyone else, it just looks like you're not working hard enough.

Build huge piles of documents around your workspace. That way, you can surf the web to your heart's content, whilst the rest of the office thinks you're buried deep in it, diligently working through your enormous workload.

To the casual observer, last year's work looks the same as today's work; it's volume that counts. Pile them high and wide.

If you know somebody is coming to your cubicle/office, bury the document you'll need halfway down in an existing stack and rummage for it when he/she arrives. You then buy yourself time for a quick assessment of the situation:

- If it's your boss and you are able to quickly locate it, you can demonstrate your Houdini-like organizational skills and look like you are extremely busy and in touch, having everything at your command;
- If it's a colleague trying to fob work off onto you, you can pretend to search everywhere for the document and just not be able to lay your hands on it at that moment. Your colleague will then think that you are either too busy or too disorganized for them to rely upon you.

Either way, it's mission accomplished!

Always appear worried

If you don't follow this rule, you will invariably have good reason to do so eventually… If you are not worried now, think of how worried you'll look when you're fired! You have everything in the world to be worried about – you could be fired tomorrow, or worse still, today! You must always be looking over your shoulder, just in case.

You see, bosses derive a sense of joy and well-being from seeing their employees in a state of eternal misery – that is why the saddest and glum looking employees get to stay.

Your mission must be to spend your entire days looking as though your dog just died.

Whereas, if you make the mistake of looking like you might be happy, contented or the least bit fulfilled with your work, nothing will improve your boss' day better than firing you and wiping that dumb smile off your face.

Remember, you are there to work – you are not there to have fun – so do not, under any circumstances, look as though you are (or even be tempted to feign happiness). If you even think about it, do so at your peril.

Always appear tired

This is a corollary of the above rule to look worried.

This look can be easily achieved by simply rubbing the eyes with the thumb and forefinger. If you wear glasses, the effect is even better! Simply, remove the glasses slowly and proceed to rub. The beauty of this for the regular eyeglass wearer, is that once you have removed the glasses, you will already look like a stunned mullet, even if it is first thing in the morning.

Remember, the idea is that you want to look like you are terribly overworked and dedicated to the company 24/7.

The effect only works if you make others think that your abject exhaustion is work-related. The technique loses much of its luster if others realize that you only managed to crawl into bed at 6 am, after a big night out.

Outsourcing responsibility

CHAPTER

9

Responsibility is poison to a career. You must be prepared to do all that you can (and then some) to avoid it.

There are various personal risk management tools available to help you achieve this – and all at the company's (enormous) expense.

It would be criminally negligent of you not to avail yourself to them, since you are not paying for them.

Cover your backside

This is a thoroughly noble goal to which you should aspire on a daily basis. It is another word for 'survival'.

If you suspect any project or undertaking in which you are:

* involved;
* associated with; or
* in which anyone who matters might even *think* you may have had the slightest involvement, you need to prepare the groundwork very early on, in order to spread the blame – preferably as far away as possible from you.

Your aim should always be to spread blame as you would a load of fresh manure on a hot summer's day – as fast as possible and as far away from you as you can.

> *"If you can smile when things go wrong, you obviously have someone in mind to blame."*

Use consultants to cover your backside

The best and most effective way to cover your backside is through the use of a consultant – or, better still, an army of them.

Consultants give you the aura of invincibility in that you can:

- get them to say anything you want, since they rely upon you for their bread and butter;
- lay the blame for all kinds of problems on them after they are gone, since they will not be around to hear it all, or, to realize you are lying through your teeth and maligning them.

Consultants are like company cars – they are able to take, in their stride, any kind of punishment that you care to dish out.

A further unpublicized benefit of consultants is that their very presence can keep all staff on their toes. They will know from their own previous unpleasant and bitter experience that consultants tend to herald the advent of further cut-backs. And, of course, cut-backs often mean a reduction in the headcount. Staff will tend to perform at their peak when they perceive the presence of a threat that could potentially put an end to their livelihood.

Often, you will find that bosses will call in consultants for no good reason other than the pure fun of seeing people squirm and quivering with fear under the burden of the speculation that the mere presence of the consultants will generate.

Keep yourself (relatively) scarce

Those in a position of power are often those who are least available for comment or presence when the occasion arises.

When we are always and instantly available, we risk becoming a little too common, or just too predictable. In some situations, a willingness to be helpful can become a handicap. When you are always available 'on tap' (or only just expected to be), you become far less appreciated and your importance diminishes.

You can become more appreciated for your expertise by not making yourself so readily available. In fact, it is crucial that you make yourself less available (up to a point).

This is one of the keys to projecting your stature and importance to others.

Volunteer staff for salary cuts

If the company cuts your salary in order to stay in business (or to help fund the lease on your boss' shiny new Lexus) you could choose to just grit your teeth, smile and take the hit 'for the good of the company', forever thankful that you still have a job.

Better yet, if others have confided to you their fear of losing their jobs (see *Rule 31*), you could suggest that instead of cutting your salary, you could present to management the names of five other staff guaranteed to meekly accept a pay cut without causing any waves, resentment or unrest.

Your value in maintaining industrial relations harmony will be seen positively by the company and may well save you from a pay cut of your own.

If executed well enough, it might actually lead to a pay increase or some other form of performance bonus, as a reward for having saved the company hundreds of thousands of dollars that could have been potentially lost in industrial unrest, PR damage and legal fees.

" When I do good, I feel good;
when I do bad, I feel better. "

You are never going to keep your job until you master the art of meetings.

The business meeting is best compared to a funeral; a gathering of people, wearing uncomfortable clothing who would rather be somewhere else. The major difference is that funerals usually have a definite purpose. If done correctly, nothing is buried once-and-for-all in a meeting.

If an idea looks dead, it is your duty to breathe life into it to ensure that it reappears at another meeting later in the year.

Remember that, if you are not engaged in meetings for most of your day, chances are that you might have to actually do some _real work_. Naturally, you will want to do all that you can to avoid that from _ever_ happening.

Make endless meetings your mission

There are two major kinds of meetings:

1. meetings held for the sake of tradition; and
2. meetings with a supposed purpose.

Meetings that are held for the sake of tradition

For example, many managers seem to like meeting in order to discuss 'corporate strategy'. This, of course, is a nonsense term. Most of the people using the term wouldn't know real 'corporate strategy' if they found it in bed with them. After, 'I love you' it is the most over-used phrase in the English language.

The 'corporate strategy' type will tell you they are busy considering the 'big-picture'. The only 'big-picture' many of them are familiar with appears every month at the newsstand; the rest of us usually refer to it as a 'centerfold'.

Their bookshelves are stocked with such erudite titles as _The Competitive_ *and Strategic Advantage of Managers who Really Know what they're Doing*. No known copy of this book has actually been read (much less, understood) by such managers.

You had better become accustomed to this type of meeting, since they account for 89% of all meetings (based on a study in which I threw darts at a board until my score sounded about right). This type of meeting operates the way 'show and tell' used to at school, with everyone having their turn at saying something. The only difference was, that at school, the kids actually had something constructive and meaningful to say.

When called upon to speak, if you are unprepared, simply say that you are still working on whatever it is that you were supposed to be working on.

These meetings are the reason most managers use to avoid having to actually work. This is why they are useful for you. The only downside is the mind-numbing boredom they generate. However, being bored beats being unemployed.

Meetings with a supposed purpose

These can be trickier, depending upon the supposed purpose. More often than not, the purpose is harmless; someone just wants to while away the hours with a PowerPoint presentation, which enables them to show-off the latest transition effects, which they spent most of yesterday downloading from the internet.

All you need to do in this kind of meeting is sit upright (whilst allowing your mind to drift in fantasy), ask for a copy of the presentation to study carefully, and then take the report back to your office and throw it away.

However, if you are a boss, you will take the presentation back to your office, write the name of the subordinate you most wish to 'needle' today, followed with a question mark: for example, "Doug?" Then you send it to that person and forget all about it for about six to nine months. At some future meeting (whilst pondering how much you dislike the way he parts his hair), you raise this again with him and ask how his report is coming along on the subject – then sit back and watch the fun…

> ## " At work, activity is often mistaken for achievement."

Walk into an office/meeting as if you own it

Projecting confidence in any work situation is vital.

It is not necessary to have any knowledge about (much less understand) what is actually going on, to be able to exude confidence – in fact, those who project the most confidence are usually the ones with the least to be confident about.

Confidence is a learned reaction, in much the same way as the learned responses of Pavlov's dog. If it doesn't come naturally to you, you must practice it.

Do those with more confidence know more than you? Are they better than you? Of course not. In fact the contrary is usually the case. *Confidence has absolutely nothing to do with skill, ability or talent.* It is more about chutzpah.

Keep practising the skill until an attitude of confidence becomes part of your very nature; an instinctive reaction on your part.

You'll know when you've arrived when someone comes to you after a meeting and says: "How did you know those GDP figures for the last 10 years from off the top of your head?"

You'll, of course, be thinking to yourself "and you believed that?"

It's all about bluff and bull dust.

> ## " Confidence has absolutely nothing to do with skill, ability or talent. "

Ultimate plan
for success

CHAPTER
11

This section is only for the politicians' politician – that is, for the political virtuoso. It is the advanced course. Gentle souls and kind-hearted family types need not continue.

If your thirst for money and power was not quenched by the preceding chapters, then you are a member of the most elite class of corporate scumbags. You not only want to have your cake and eat it too, but you also want (and need):

- to fire the chef and everyone else in the kitchen who actually made the cake;
- to have everyone else's cake and eat it too; and
- if for some reason you can't have someone's cake, you want to poison it.

Only a rare breed gets to make it this far. The picture you might have in your mind of such a creature may be a pulsating, drooling character who stalks the corporate corridors carrying a blood-soaked machete. Quite the opposite is true, in fact.

It's the mild mannered ones who, seemingly, wouldn't tread on an ant, that you most need to watch out for.

Those who try most to avoid open confrontation, are usually the ones who tend to wreak the most havoc and destruction using an indirect and non-confrontational approach.

When all else fails ... use blackmail

When the worst happens and your being fired is unavoidable, if you agree that 'the ends justifies the means' and that 'all's fair...', you could always consider resorting to the tactic used by Lester Burnham (the lead character played by Kevin Spacey in the Academy Award winning film, *American Beauty*).

He *blackmailed* his boss for a massively increased severance package.

It is worth noting that some may regard the use of blackmail as an ethically questionable practice. Others have even gone so far as to suggest that it may even be illegal to do so. Naturally, this is a decision that must be left to the individual to decide according to one's own conscience (and that person's taste for prison food…).

"The brain is a wonderful thing — it never stops working from the moment we wake until we set foot in the office."

And finally, the single best way to keep your job…

Fire everyone and then re-employ yourself

You can only use this guaranteed fail-safe technique if you have religiously followed all of the other rules for years. This may sound so far-fetched and crazy, that no-one could possibly ever fall for it – however, I have actually seen it done!

This technique consists of devising a grand cost-saving plan to make your entire department/division/office redundant and to outsource all of its functions. You must recklessly disregard the fact that such outsourcing will ultimately triple the company's expenses and maximize inconvenience and disruption to the proper functioning of the business and to the remaining management.

The trick is to assemble a set of numbers solely emphasizing the massive short-term gains achieved and ignoring all down-sides.

The best time to put forward such a plan is when the corporate head office is experiencing a major crisis, so that your idea will seem like small potatoes and not attract too much attention or scrutiny. The idea of generating such immediate cost-savings will prove too good to resist and will ensure that the plan is pushed through and approved, without too much scrutiny. In the frenzy, no one will notice that the short-term gains will continue for no longer than about two to three months and that the plan makes absolutely no long-term sense for the company.

Following is a summary of the steps you need to take (and hurdles to overcome) to put such a plan into action:

- The success of the plan relies upon an emphasis on the savings generated and the benefit to the company's bottom line, *beginning from next month*. You need to back this plan up with numbers – regardless of how spurious or misleading they might be. The more ridiculous they appear, showing humongous and fantastic savings, the more likely they are to be accepted.

- If the company is a publicly listed one, the above step is critical. This is because it caters to the market's demands that companies downsize and it gives those pesky analysts the rich swag of employee scalps on a plate, they always seem to be craving. The company hits a home run and you are a hero!

- Allocate yourself a rich severance package (you get to do this because you are the architect of the close-down plan). That is why carefully planning the numbers is such an important step – you need to allocate enough money to be able to make a fat severance payment to yourself.

- Screwing the other employees out of the bulk of their entitlements and using those savings to nicely feather your own nest, can achieve a *double bonus* for yourself. You have an easy run here, since the other employees are going to be powerless to do anything about it. Politically, they will have no weight within the organization, as everyone will already know they are on their way out – and dead employees tell no tales.

- Nominate a trusted crony (preferably one devoid of talent, stature and of the respect of others), who poses no threat to you, to implement the plan. Give them a severance package that is more money than they could ever earn on their own merits anywhere else – this will ensure they never ask the blindingly obvious question on everyone's mind: *How can any of this make any sense?*

Now comes the real beauty of the plan:

- Naturally, once you have sold the plan to head office, you make your exit as fast as you can and collect the pot of gold you have set aside for yourself. End your tenure before everyone else is gone. You will, thereby, be able to spare your tender soul from having to witness first-hand the pathetic and messy goodbyes, the tears and personal devastation and upheaval that you have inflicted upon the others.

- Once the plan is irrevocably in motion and head office finally realizes the stupidity of the idea, it will ask you to stay on as a consultant to ensure the process is managed to its conclusion – note that this relies heavily on the notion that head office sees your 2IC as a total nincompoop and would do anything to have you back.

- And here's the punch line… not only do you get to 'manage' the close down process, but you also collect another hefty sum for yourself in 'consulting fees'. The sum total of your efforts here will consist of no more than holding the door open for those being fired (and delivering the final push out the door to them), whilst delegating the grunt-work to your 2IC – this will allow you the quiet time you need to tend to your hobby farm whilst being handsomely paid.

- As soon as it becomes apparent that the closedown should never have happened, you allow yourself to be persuaded to stick around as a part-time consultant on 90% of your old salary, to ensure that the company retains the benefit of your counsel and experience. This allows the company to triumphantly announce to the market that it has successfully avoided a _brain-drain_ of talent, by minimizing the loss of intellectual capital that the company has so carefully (and expensively) cultivated and accumulated. Many analysts will drool with glee while penning the 'strong buy' recommendations they will be issuing, on the strength of these assurances by management.

If you can't slither your way out of the entire process without having snaffled for yourself, at least:

- several million dollars in cash (after taxes);
- a shiny new Range Rover loaded to the bull-bar with options;
- a couple of the latest notebook computers;
- the snazziest and most expensive mobile phones;
- gadgets galore for your entire family;
- a nice set of choice season football tickets for you and your friends;
- lots of other luscious and expensive company-funded perks and memberships,

... then you haven't really applied your mind creatively to the task and have badly let yourself down.

Never mind though, as all is not lost. You can always repeat the effort and do it better… at your next job.

"The last person who quit or was fired can conveniently be held responsible for everything that goes (or ever went) wrong."

CHAPTER

12

conclusion and revision quiz

You will notice that all the above rules have one underlying factor in common; they are all designed to give you a certain image. Image is what you live and die by in the corporate world.

Since you have learned that *bad things happen to good people*, there is no future in being 'good'.

Remember that it is your duty to your employer to keep yourself from being over-loaded with work – because when you are, you are unable to produce the quality work you take pride in.

Hence, constantly looking for shortcuts, delegating and shirking responsibility is not only ethical, but obligatory, as a conscientious and diligent employee.

You must avoid work-induced stress at all costs – after all, you are no good to your employer if you die of a heart attack. The single best way to achieve this goal is by avoiding any form of work at all costs.

Tactics that are over-used are no longer tactics – broaden your repertoire and surprise everyone!

Once you have a job, you need to keep it – this is not easy.

The paradox of keeping your job

Trying to keep your job is a veritable high-wire juggling act (with no safety net below you). In order to keep your job, you need to:

    … blend in with the team, but stand out from the pack;
    … be happy, but look worried;
    … not conform, but not rock the boat;
    … consider all options, but stay focused;
    … communicate with colleagues, but don't talk about your problems;
    … make your colleagues your family, but keep your personal life to yourself;

… be interested in the plight of your colleagues, but not care about them;

… be altruistic, but look out for number 1.

Following *all* these rules will ensure that you reach a position of power in the corporate world and get to experience and enjoy the all trappings of success.

The best part is that you will not have to concern yourself with sharing any of that success with friends (because you won't have any left). Your spouse won't know you, because she will have long since run off with the pool-cleaner or the gardener (or, in extreme cases, with both of them).

Your children won't recognize you, but you will have provided for them all of the essential things that love just cannot buy: bikes, computers, designer clothes and flashy cars.

Whenever your personal life takes a nosedive, rest assured that your work life will provide you with all the comfort and warmth you require… during business hours, at least.

"Being indecisive is the key to
flexibility, or, perhaps it isn't…"

Revision quiz

This corporate quiz has been devised by a panel of experts to scientifically measure your level of comprehension of the foregoing text that you (should) have read. Score your answers as you go and rate them at the end of the quiz.

1. You intend to apply for a plum job, for which you are patently unqualified. In your resume, do you:

    (a) Tell the truth, since you are honest.
    (b) Tell the truth, since you are stupid.
    (c) Embellish a little and hope you don't get caught out.
    (d) Lie like blazes and bluff your way through it if caught.

2. At the interview you are asked your view on a subject on which you know absolutely nothing. Do you:

    (a) Admit you do not know the answer, since you are honest.
    (b) Admit you do not know the answer, since you are stupid.
    (c) Go off on a tangent and use lots of big words.
    (d) Create a diversion such as a small fire and hope they forget the question after the confusion has settled.

3. By some miracle you are offered the job. Do you:

> *(a) Thank the interviewer politely and accept the offer.*
> *(b) Thank the interviewer profusely and enthusiastically accept the offer, without enquiring about the compensation package.*
> *(c) Insist on signing an employment contract on the same day, before they have a chance to find any of your prison records.*
> *(d) Accept the offer verbally and then later (once the other candidates have been informed that the job is taken), demand a huge sign-on bonus and a lavish compensation package. Threaten them with a lawsuit if they refuse to cave in to your demands.*

4. After only the second day on the job, you discover that your boss has embezzled $1 million dollars from the company. Do you:

> *(a) Blow the whistle because it's the honest thing to do.*
> *(b) Blow the whistle and get fired because it's the stupid thing to do.*
> *(c) Discretely inform your boss that you know what she is up to and will blow the whistle unless she splits the money with you.*
> *(d) Blow the whistle on your boss by announcing that she has embezzled $100,000, only after you have figured out a foolproof way of pocketing the other $900,000.*

5. You happen upon photos of the CEO in a compromising position with a secretary and a small furry pet. Do you:

> *(a) Destroy them because they are disgusting.*
> *(b) Destroy them because you are stupid.*
> *(c) Discretely threaten to show them to his wife and children unless he agrees to help you slither up the corporate ladder.*
> *(d) Post them on the company's website in the 'latest news' section.*

6. You are confronted by the corporate regulator with irrefutable evidence of you profiting from insider trading in your company's shares. You purchased a large parcel of shares in your name prior to an important announcement, driving the stock price massively upwards. Do you:

> *(a) Admit everything and offer to repay the money.*
> *(b) Deny everything and offer to repay the money.*
> *(c) Offer to sell the shares immediately and split the profits, in return for all charges being dropped, or deal on a lower sentence of weekend detention.*
> *(d) Admit that you purchased the shares at the direction of your boss and that you are fronting a secret trust set up for her and the entire board of directors. Offer to give evidence against them all in return for immunity from prosecution and a handsome reward.*

7. You are given the task of dismissing a long-serving employee, on the grounds of redundancy. Your only brief is to do it properly. Do you:

> *(a) Take that person into your office, break the news gently, offer a generous severance package, outplacement assistance and an appropriate send-off.*
> *(b) Break the news gently and offer the legal minimum severance package.*
> *(c) Send an email to the person concerned announcing that effective from the close of business today, they are out of a job.*
> *(d) Whilst the person concerned is on leave, have your secretary send them an email announcing that effective from the close of business today, they are out of a job. Cc a copy of the message to everyone else in the company.*

8. You discover that a co-worker is being paid more than you. Do you:

> *(a) Grin and bear it. After all, that's life.*
> *(b) Grit your teeth and bear it. Your time will come.*
> *(c) Demand an immediate review of your salary and benefits package.*
> *(d) Find a way to have that co-worker publicly humiliated, fired and jailed. Then demand an immediate review of your salary and benefits package.*

9. Your typical workday lunch consists of:

> *(a) The contents of the brown paper bag that your husband packs for you.*
> *(b) A greasy burger and fries from the nearest fast-food outlet.*
> *(c) Lunch at a restaurant with a friend of your choice, under the guise of a client lunch, claimed back on your company expense account.*
> *(d) Five lavish courses of the finest cuisine, wine, brandy and port (followed by cigars), at the finest five star establishments, where the waiters are better dressed than you. Followed by an afternoon siesta in a suite at the Grand Ritz – all on the corporate credit card.*

10. Do you regard your corporate expense account as:

> *(a) A privilege granted to you, to be used frugally and sparingly, because you are honest.*
> *(b) A privilege granted to you, to be used frugally and sparingly because you are stupid.*
> *(c) A status symbol to be used and abused as much as is legally possible.*
> *(d) Your own personal bank with unlimited funds available, whose availability and use for personal expenses is limited only by your imagination, daring and creativity.*

Rate your score

Scoring
For every question where you selected answer A award yourself 1 point.
For every question where you selected answer B award yourself 2 points.
For every question where you selected answer C award yourself 10 points.
For every question where you selected answer D award yourself 20 points.

If your score was…

10 points or less

Don't worry about giving up your day job, because others are working on it for you. It is best that you not make any plans at work that depend on you keeping your job beyond the next tea break. You have obviously skipped the rest of this book and jumped straight to this quiz.

20 points or less

You are a plodder with no aspirations or ambition. You are destined to be driving a $1500 car for the rest of your life. The life expectancy of your career can be measured with an egg timer. You must hurry and re-read this book – v e r y carefully!

21–100 points

You have the makings of a high-flyer. There are sparks of creativity that will be noticed. However, don't rest on your laurels, you need to work hard to become more of a scumbag, in order to succeed. There are parts of this book that you didn't take in and certain morals that you have not yet tossed aside. Re-read this book thoroughly.

101–200 points

You are a consummate corporate politician. You place no value on morals, family, scruples or fair play. Well done! Give this book another quick once-over and you should be OK.

201–1000 points

You are a lying, cheating scoundrel – and obviously a political virtuoso. It is always easy to spot someone who has carefully read and understood all of the lessons contained within this book. You are a grand master of corporate thuggery, destined to become a future chairman of the board (as soon as the next wave of corporate arrests and convictions frees up that spot for you).

"Youth and enthusiasm are no match for experience and treachery."

The last remaining rule

Since you've paid for the full 60 rules, we didn't want you to feel short-changed by a missing out on one, so here it is…

 Use paranoia as a tool for survival

Andrew Grove the chairman of semiconductor manufacturer Intel once famously quipped that "only the paranoid survive". He was right. You need to stay paranoid — because *everyone* is out to get you.

If it's good enough for Andy Grove to feel this way, then it's sure good enough for you — and *you* are decidedly *not* Andy Grove.

If you hadn't already gotten the message though the other 59 rules then you might as well quietly put this book down and start writing your resignation … right NOW.

Just imagine if Caesar had sussed out Brutus a little sooner. Had he read this book, he would have known to spend more time at the Senatorial water cooler to get the latest gossip about Brutus' plans. However, he did not. He discovered that Brutus was not such a dumb 2IC after all … via the end of a very sharp knife.

Afterword

As a captain of industry, I am indeed flattered to have been invited to compose a few words of encouragement to readers who wish to improve themselves and their job prospects.

It's always important to understand loyalty to your boss – I especially liked the fact that the author has devoted an entire chapter to 'showing your boss the respect he deserves'. I've always shown loyalty to my boss, and this has got me to where I am today. I am living proof that you don't need an Eye Vee League university or one of those NBA's to succeed as a manager.

One day, when I finally gain some respite from my heavy round of board meetings and committees, I fully intend to read this textbook. I trust that the author has parlayed the experiences gained working under me into this fine academic work advancing the study of management science.

As a career mentor, I spent an unusual amount of the time with the author teaching him the ropes and anointing him with the benefit of my considerable experience in the field of business and management. This kind of experience cannot be bought or found in any college.

Upon briefly scanning the book, I am indeed heartened by the author's decision to dedicate a considerable portion of this work to the unsung heroes of the corporate world – the second in command (2IC). It is with great pride that I can say that I have had the skill and foresight to be able to count myself as one. 2ICs are to be found silently and willingly propping up any organization in distress, whilst allowing the CEO to take all the credit.

Not everyone has the requisite traits to be handpicked by a CEO for this important role. I work almost every day to help deliver the promise.

I trust you will have found this a valuable addition to your library to both extend your learning in the craft of management and enhance your career prospects in the corporate world.

Ivan

I.M.A. Dumass
Vice President (and the author's former boss)

About the author

The author is a battle-scarred veteran of corporate politics and the dictatorships of any number of wannabe Stalins. He has long since abandoned (or been abandoned by?) full-time corporate life. Although he occasionally still dreams of becoming editor of *MAD* magazine.

Despite the setbacks, he made it to the TOP and is now ready to show you how you can do the same.

He found the vast majority of those he worked with over the years to be wonderful and competent people. Alas, amongst them there was the occasional bonehead (you know who you are).

How to
Lie,
Cheat & Steal
Your Way to the *TOP*

www.lazyexecutive.com